The Pursuit of BRAVE

Fear-Less, Live More:
Embracing BRAVE in Daily Life

Michelle Lee Graham   Jacquilyn Banta

The Pursuit of BRAVE

Fear-Less, Live More: Embracing Brave in Daily Life

Copyright© 2024 Michelle Lee Graham & Jacquilyn Banta.
ALL RIGHTS RESERVED.

No part of this book, or its associated ancillary materials may be reproduced or transmitted in any form or by any means, electronic or mechanical, including photocopying, recording, or by any informational storage or retrieval system without permission from the publisher.

Editor: Alexa Tanen
Format: Rocio Monroy
Photographer: Stephanie Adkisson

Dedication

The Pursuit of BRAVE is dedicated to the courageous and selfless parents who embody bravery in the face of life's greatest challenges. It honors those who have endured the unimaginable pain of losing a child far too soon, their hearts forever bearing the weight of that profound absence. It celebrates the parents who lead with strength and tenderness, tirelessly advocating for their children's needs and well-being against all odds. These BRAVE parents pour every ounce of their love and resources into giving their sons and daughters the best possible life.

Day after day, they fearlessly give of themselves, pushing through exhaustion and adversity to be the unwavering rocks their children can always count on. Behind closed doors, these resilient parents wage silent battles against their own scars, determined to shield their innocent children from inheriting wounds that do not belong to them.

The Pursuit of BRAVE recognizes the awe-inspiring mothers who chose life for their babies even when it meant having to say goodbye and those who carry the bittersweet memory of tiny heartbeats that never had the chance to grow outside the safety of the womb. In a world that often overlooks the everyday acts of heroism that define parenthood, this dedication stands as a testament to the extraordinary BRAVE parents who shape the future through their boundless love and fearlessness.

Introduction

Navigating BRAVE choices means **Being Resilient, Authentic, Vulnerable, and Empowered**, and it is a delicate balancing act. It requires us to thoughtfully consider the risks. These types of choices are not always easy. They often involve stepping outside our comfort zones and embracing uncertainty. However, we can unlock our true potential through BRAVE and cultivate lives of purpose and fulfillment.

Resilience allows us to bounce back from setbacks and challenges, while authenticity ensures we are true to ourselves and our values. Vulnerability opens the door to deeper connections and personal growth as we courageously share our authentic selves. When we choose from a place of empowerment, **we reclaim ourselves and take control of our destinies**.

Though the path may be riddled with obstacles and difficult decisions, the rewards of navigating BRAVE choices are immense. By embracing this framework, we can navigate the complexities of life with courage, self-awareness, and a steadfast commitment to our highest good. The journey requires vulnerability, grit, and a willingness to take calculated risks. Still, the personal transformation and sense of purpose that emerges from this process are truly invaluable.

BRAVE: Be

Being BRAVE is so much more than a fleeting feeling or a momentary act of courage. It's a mindset, a way of living that permeates every aspect of your life. To truly be brave is to embrace the core principles - Being Resilient, Authentic, Vulnerable, and Empowered. It's about making intentional and conscious choices each and every day with a BRAVE mentality.

This means being deliberate and purposeful in our thoughts, words, and actions, refusing to passively let life happen but instead proactively shaping it. It's about cultivating an unwavering inner strength and flexibility to bounce back from setbacks, adapt to change, and keep moving forward despite fear or adversity.

Bravery also requires vulnerability to show up as your authentic self, remove your masks, and let others see the messy, imperfect humanity underneath. It demands the empowerment to own your power, to have the courage of your convictions, and to unapologetically pursue your dreams and goals.

Far from a one-time feat, BRAVE is a daily practice, a commitment to living with intention in every moment. It's choosing courage over comfort, authenticity over conformity, and growth over stagnation. In these everyday choices, we build the mental, emotional, and spiritual muscle to tackle life's biggest challenges. True bravery is not a temporary state but a way of being that permeates and empowers every facet of your existence.

Be Decisive

The art of intentionality when making choices is a powerful practice that can profoundly transform our lives. At its core, it involves approaching each decision with a heightened sense of awareness and purpose rather than simply reacting on autopilot. When we cultivate intentionality, we step back and carefully consider the potential implications and consequences of our choices, both for ourselves and those around us.

This requires us to tune inward, get in touch with our values, priorities, and long-term goals, and make selections that align with our deepest selves. It's about being present in the moment, considering multiple perspectives, and making conscious, deliberate selections - even for the seemingly small, mundane daily choices. By practicing intentionality, we take back our power of self and avoid mindlessly drifting through life.

We become the architects of our experiences, thoughtfully shaping our paths forward with each decision. This level of mindfulness can be challenging at first. Still, with time and dedication, it becomes a natural way of being that imbues our lives with greater meaning, fulfillment, and a profound sense of personal integrity. The art of intentionality is a transformative skill that allows us to live with greater purpose, authenticity, and alignment with our deepest values.

> We become the architects of our experiences, thoughtfully shaping our paths forward with each decision.

The late Walt Disney was a true master of intentionality, and this meticulous attention to detail is palpable the moment you step foot into Disneyland. Every element, from the whimsical architecture lining Main Street to the precisely manicured landscaping and the enchanting background music piped throughout, has been carefully curated.

Disney was a visionary who understood the power of immersion could profoundly shape the guest experience. Nothing was left to chance - every color, every texture, every hidden Mickey was strategically placed to transport visitors into the magical worlds of Disney's imagination. Even the trash cans and park benches were designed with an eye for aesthetics, blending seamlessly into the meticulously crafted environments.

This unyielding commitment to intentionality has allowed Disneyland to maintain its timeless allure and captivate generations of guests, who find themselves willingly losing touch with reality as they become fully enveloped in Disney's meticulously constructed realms of wonder and delight. It is a testament to Walt Disney's visionary leadership and the enduring power of his creative genius that even the most minor details within his beloved park continue to be imbued with such purpose and meaning.

Be Alive

Living with intentionality, resilience, authenticity, and vulnerability is the essence of BRAVE living. It is a way of being that requires great courage and self-awareness, but the rewards are immense. When we approach life intentionally, we are deliberate and thoughtful in our actions, aligning our choices with our deepest values and beliefs.

This unwavering sense of purpose provides a steady foundation, even as we navigate the ups and downs of life. Resilience becomes a superpower - the ability to bend without breaking, weather the storms, and emerge stronger on the other side. Authenticity is the bedrock upon which this BRAVE living is built; it is the practice of honoring our true selves, letting go of pretenses and facades.

Vulnerability - that tender openness to experience - is the portal through which we access our greatest growth and connection. Far from weakness, vulnerability takes immense bravery, for it requires us to shed the protective layers and reveal our imperfect selves. This BRAVE living, with all its demands, ultimately cultivates a profound sense of empowerment.

When we live with intention, resilience, authenticity, and vulnerability, we tap into an unwavering inner strength to meet life's challenges head-on. We become agents of our transformation. We evolve and expand in ways that enrich not just our own lives but the lives of all those we encounter. **BRAVE living is a revolutionary act of self-determination, a bold declaration that we will not merely exist but truly live.**

> BRAVE living is a revolutionary act of self-determination, a bold declaration that we will not merely exist but truly live.

Living bravely is not just a noble idea but a necessary practice in a world that often fails to accommodate the diverse range of human minds and experiences. As one author knows, having a child with autism was a transformative experience that shifted her perspective.

Rather than expecting her child to conform to a world designed for the typical mind, she made the BRAVE choice to reshape that world to better serve her son's unique needs. Too often, we resign ourselves to simply existing within the confines of a society that prioritizes conformity and sameness.

But real courage lies in challenging those norms. A child with autism may see sounds as colors or hear the world in a fundamentally distinct way - and that is not a weakness to overcome but a gift to honor.

So often, we become consumed with micromanaging the actions and behaviors of our friends, family members, coworkers, and even strangers in a desperate attempt to maintain a sense of order and security in our lives. We may criticize their choices, impose our will on their decisions, or even manipulate situations to ensure things go our way. However, this futile quest to control others only robs us of our power and autonomy.

When we relinquish the need to govern the lives of those around us, we free up mental and emotional bandwidth to focus inward, examine our thoughts, feelings, and behaviors, and make conscious choices that align with our values and priorities. It is only by releasing our tight grip on the people and circumstances outside our control that we can truly seize the reins of our own existence, crafting the life we want to live rather than the one we feel forced into.

The irony is that the more we try to control others, the less control we have over our own lives - but by letting go of that need, we unlock the door to self-mastery and the freedom to direct our own path forward. **The fastest way to gain**

> **The fastest way to gain control of your life is to stop controlling everyone around you.**

By living bravely and embracing our differences, we don't just benefit those with unique needs. We all stand to gain a richer, more vibrant, and more compassionate world. When we let go of the idea that there is a single right way to be and instead welcome the full spectrum of human diversity, we open ourselves up to new modes of thinking, feeling, and experiencing that can elevate and transform us all.

True progress happens not by forcing everyone to fit a mold but by radically reimagining that mold to accommodate the boundless creativity and potential within each of us. This is the essence of brave living - to see the world not as it is but as it could be.

Be Purposeful

Living out your purpose is a profound calling that goes beyond just personal fulfillment - it is a divine, sacred mission entrusted to us by the Creator himself. The authors believe God has intentionally crafted each individual with a specific purpose, endowing us with unique gifts, passions, convictions, and strengths meant to be leveraged for His greater good.

When we take the time to truly understand ourselves - our natural talents, the causes that stir our hearts, the beliefs that shape our moral compasses, and the abilities that empower us - we unlock our purposes. This self-awareness allows us to stop aimlessly searching and focus on our callings.

Rather than getting caught up in the noise of worldly distractions and confused ambitions, we can home in on how we are meant to serve and glorify God. It may be through bringing people to Him, championing causes, leveraging our professional skills, or simply modeling Christ's character in our everyday lives.

Fulfilling this divine purpose may require sacrifice, humility, and obedience, but the eternal rewards and spiritual fulfillment from aligning our lives with God's will are immeasurable. When we commit to living out our God-given purposes, we find joy.

Do you believe that when you pursue purpose and mission with passion and integrity, the money will follow? Over the years, we've encountered numerous opportunities to provide programs or family support that did not align with our commitments to treating clients with integrity, respect, and dignity.

For example, we were once offered $100,000 to support our Heart to Home Resource Closet. It provides new clothing, diapers, hygiene kits, and other essentials for children and youth in the foster system. The space is designed to be welcoming and dignified, allowing children experiencing trauma to choose items they feel comfortable with.

However, the potential funder suggested saving money by moving from a boutique-style environment to a warehouse storage unit. Only then would they provide the funding. This proposal conflicted with the core values of offering dignity and respect to foster youth.

Staying true to the mission, we respectfully declined the offer. We remained committed to providing dignity and support to foster youth. As a result, we have since received over $1 million in resources that continue to support the foster youth in our community, all while upholding our values of respect and dignity.

This is just one of many examples of how we prioritize purpose over profit.

Chasing the purpose, not the money, is a crucial mindset shift that can lead to profound fulfillment and success. Rather than fixating on financial gain as the ultimate goal, this approach encourages us to seek out work, hobbies, and lifestyle choices that are deeply meaningful and aligned with our core values and passions.

Purpose-driven work is often in high demand, provides immense intrinsic satisfaction, and taps into our greatest strengths and talents. Moreover, the drive to keep growing, learning, and making a difference can be a far more sustainable source of motivation than the fleeting high of material acquisition.

Of course, financial stability is important and necessary. Still, when it becomes the sole driving force, we risk losing touch with our authentic selves and the profound sense of meaning that comes from living with intention. There has to be a point when your needs are met, and you can say, "This is enough."

By liberating ourselves from the constant pressure to earn and buy more beyond our needs, we open the door to a life of greater joy, impact, and true prosperity - one where we are energized by our sense of purpose rather than depleted by the mindless pursuit of wealth. This clarity of focus allows us to make wiser choices, forge deeper connections, and ultimately leave a lasting positive mark on the world around us.

Living with purpose is far greater than merely existing; it is about creating a legacy of integrity and impact that endures beyond our lifetimes.

Fear-Less BRAVE Reflection Notes

Today, I commit to Be:

BRAVE: Resilient

The remarkable phenomenon of neuroplasticity is truly astonishing, showcasing the incredible resilience and adaptability of the human brain. From the earliest moments of our lives, our brains demonstrate an astounding capacity for growth and change, rapidly forging new neural pathways.

In the first five years alone, our neurons form over a million new connections every second, laying the groundwork for a lifetime of learning, memory, and cognitive development. This process continues well into our mid-to-late twenties as the brain remains in a state of dynamic flux, constantly rewiring and reorganizing itself in response to our experiences.

Even more remarkably, the brain's neuroplasticity allows it to bounce back from adversity and trauma. When we face significant challenges or upheaval in our lives, the brain's resilience enables it to adapt and rebuild, rerouting neural connections and finding new ways to process information and respond to stimuli. Rather than becoming rigidly fixed or permanently damaged, the brain possesses an almost miraculous capacity to heal in the face of adversity.

Each time we navigate life challenges, we build our resilience. People come from diverse backgrounds; some may have faced deep, lifelong trauma, while others may have grown up in nurturing environments with fewer hurdles. Yet, resilience is developed in both scenarios.

One does not need to experience profound loss, injury, abuse, or grief to learn resilience; it can also be cultivated in a supportive environment.

The concept of trauma and healing is often misunderstood. Imagine a clear glass of water - pure, clean, and refreshing. But then, imagine adding a spoonful of mud to that water. The once-clear liquid is now murky and clouded, no matter how much sugar you try to add. The mud remains, disrupting the purity of the water.

> Trauma is an independent entity, a metaphorical mud contaminating our emotional and psychological well-being. around you.

This is akin to how trauma operates within the human psyche. Trauma is an independent entity, a metaphorical mud contaminating our emotional and psychological well-being. No amount of positivity, self-improvement, or sugar can simply remove that trauma. It persists, stubbornly tainting our inner landscape until it is directly addressed and extracted.

To truly heal from trauma, whether physical or emotional, requires a multi-faceted approach. First, creating a sense of safety and stability is paramount, allowing the brain's neuroplasticity to facilitate real change. Second, developing emotional awareness and regulating intense feelings is crucial. And finally, reclaiming your true identity - separate from the trauma - empowers authentic growth and healing. Only by addressing trauma at its root can we hope to remove the mud and restore our clarity.

Resilience is not the absence of hardship but the strength to overcome it.

Resilient Thoughts

The power of BRAVE thoughts should not be underestimated. These four simple yet profound principles can unlock our resiliency, allowing us to break free from the constraints of faulty, self-defeating thought patterns. Resilience is the foundation, giving us the fortitude to weather life's storms and bounce back from setbacks.

Far too many people become their own worst enemies, sabotaging opportunities simply because they are trapped in a cycle of defensive, limiting beliefs. But by consciously cultivating BRAVE thoughts, we can short-circuit this self-destructive process and rewire our minds for growth, healing, and fulfilling our deepest life purposes.

It's a simple yet remarkably effective tool. Whenever a negative thought arises, counter it immediately with three positive, affirming thoughts. This conscious mental reprogramming takes practice, but it becomes second nature over time, transforming our outlooks. With BRAVE thoughts as our guide, we can learn to get out of our way and unlock our true, limitless potential.

Our thoughts wield significant power over our actions. They influence our emotions, moods, and every decision we make. While we can control our thoughts and let them guide our choices, it's also important to acknowledge that some thoughts are fleeting and should be released. BRAVE thoughts challenge negative notions, such as the belief that vulnerability equates to weakness or that betrayal defines you. These are not truths. Instead, embrace thoughts that reflect reality and empower you.

Failure does not define you; it is merely a part of the journey. When setbacks occur, pick yourself up and move forward. You are not solely defined by your actions, successes, or failures. However, if you let your thoughts define you, ensure they do so through a lens of positivity and truth.

BRAVE thoughts enable you to see beyond temporary setbacks and embrace a narrative of resilience and growth. You can shape a life defined by courage, authenticity, and bravery by consciously choosing thoughts that uplift and inspire.

One example to live by is assuming positive intent. When we assume positive intent, we keep our thoughts positive and believe others mean well. Maintaining control of your thoughts not only challenges you to be better but also inspires and encourages others to see the positivity within you.

Maintaining BRAVE thoughts allows us to rise above what the world may tell us and remain true to ourselves. Get out of your head, stay strong, and control your thoughts. Give them only the power they deserve, and if they aren't moving you forward, let them go.

Resilient Mindfulness

As children, we were largely left unequipped with the knowledge and tools to understand and manage our own emotions, mental states, and overall psychological health. We didn't talk about it because we didn't have the words.

The concepts of emotional regulation, cultivating positive thought patterns, and tending to our inner lives were not emphasized in the way they are today. However, as we've matured and gained a deeper understanding of the human psyche, we now recognize just how critical these aspects of self-care are - not just for our own well-being but for setting up the next generation for success.

Whereas our parents and grandparents may have lacked the awareness and resources to address emotions properly, we now have a wealth of research, therapeutic modalities, and educational frameworks that shed light on the profound impact our thoughts, feelings, and coping mechanisms can have on our overall quality of life. We understand that emotional regulation - the ability to recognize, process, and respond to our emotions in healthy ways - is a skill that can and should be nurtured from a young age.

Similarly, we know that adopting constructive mindsets, practicing self-compassion, and developing strong emotional intelligence are all instrumental in fostering mental resilience and thriving. Armed with this knowledge, we are now empowered to provide our children with the guidance to build a strong foundation of mental and emotional well-being - something our younger selves may have deeply benefited from.

As we integrate these principles into our lives, we can lead by example and create a culture of openness, self-awareness, and holistic health that can be passed down for generations to come.

By cultivating a BRAVE mindset, we can navigate the ebbs and flows of life with steadfast resolve, navigating uncertainty with grace, and embracing the richness that comes from authentically embracing the full spectrum of the human condition. It is a transformative journey that enhances personal growth and inspires others to embark on their own paths of self-discovery and empowerment.

Resilient Decisions

Truly BRAVE and strategic decision-makers know the immense power that lies in carefully timed pauses and moments of reflection. Knee-jerk, emotionally charged responses that many people default to are rarely the most accurate, productive, or beneficial ways to make important choices. Emotional decision-making, while tempting in the heat of the moment, can end up causing deep and lasting damage to personal and professional relationships.

The wisest understand that taking that crucial beat to breathe, considering all angles, and responding thoughtfully rather than reactively separates good decisions from disastrous ones. This strategic pause, or "power of the pause," allows you to tap into your logical faculties and override the primal urge to lash out.

By cultivating this discipline, BRAVE decision-makers can make choices that serve their best interests. While it may feel uncomfortable or counterintuitive in the moment, this willingness to pause, reflect, and respond deliberately rather than impulsively is a potent tool that helps them navigate complex personal and professional landscapes with finesse.

Fear-Less BRAVE Reflection
Notes

I am celebrating my Resiliency in:

BRAVE: Authentic

Embracing authenticity in your life journey requires a deep understanding of the self, an unwavering commitment to personal growth, and the courage to unapologetically showcase your unique qualities. Being authentic is not about carelessly disregarding social norms or using them as excuses for poor behavior. Rather, it is an approach to living as an imperfect human, acknowledging everyone's strengths and areas needing improvement with honesty and humility.

Truly authentic individuals know themselves well. They own these aspects of their identity, refusing to conform to external expectations or societal pressures. This allows them to contribute to their communities in meaningful, genuine ways, sharing their varied perspectives without fear of judgment.

Authenticity is not about perfection but the willingness to be vulnerable, learn and evolve, and show up as your truest self. By embracing this authentic approach, individuals can navigate life's challenges and opportunities with confidence, clarity, and the freedom to become their best selves.

Authentic Relationships

The goal is to cultivate real, lasting connections that go far beyond the superficial. These authentic relationships are characterized by individuals who do not compete for recognition, attention, or reward. Instead, they focus on uplifting one another, drawing attention, praise, and opportunities for ongoing growth and success.

The authors regularly reference the successful completion of tasks or receipt of awards as joint endeavors, using "we" statements to highlight collaboration. For example, "We just completed the first draft of the grant," "We have increased the overall agency budget by 15%," and "We initiated a new program." Demonstrating collaboration and presenting a unified front to their team and community. This fosters an environment of committed buy-in on decision-making and confidence in united leadership with an aligned purpose.

Encouragement is key. Team members are given opportunities to take risks and let their imaginations innovate and create. When BRAVE leadership is present, team members have the freedom to expand their skills, knowledge, and innovation in ways that propel organizations beyond their natural boundaries.

Encouraging the team to step out of their comfort zones creates opportunities for the organization to reach new

> When life inevitably brings crisis, chaos, communication breakdowns, mistakes, or relational conflicts, this cushion is a vital source of stability and resilience.

heights. A team member has an innovative idea for improving a process but is unsure about its feasibility. In a BRAVE relationship, leadership encourages this, providing resources and support to test it out. This encouragement not only boosts the individual's confidence but also opens new avenues for the organization's growth.

The concept of a Relational Cushion is a crucial aspect of human connection and support. This metaphorical cushion represents the foundation of trust, understanding, and mutual investment built between two individuals over time. When life inevitably brings crisis, chaos, communication breakdowns, mistakes, or relational conflicts, this cushion is a vital source of stability and resilience.

It acts as a protective barrier, absorbing the impact of such challenges and preventing them from completely destabilizing the relationship. Cultivating a strong relational cushion requires intentional effort and dedication from both parties. This involves actively listening, empathizing, offering compassion, and consistently nurturing the connection.

As this cushion grows thicker and more resilient through shared experiences and mutual care, it provides a sense of security that allows individuals to weather the storms of life together. Rather than crumbling under pressure, the relationship can flex and bend.

This foundation of trust and understanding becomes a reliable safety net, enabling partners to navigate difficulties more easily and emerge even stronger on the other side. The relational cushion represents the investment of time, energy, and emotional vulnerability that binds two people together, creating a foundation of support

> This foundation of trust and understanding becomes a reliable safety net, enabling partners to navigate difficulties more easily and emerge even stronger on the other side.

that can withstand the unpredictable nature of human relationships.

BRAVE relationships inspire individuals to be their best, encouraging them to dig deep within themselves and pursue the dreams and passions that motivate and uplift others. Inspired individuals are creative, innovative, and supportive of new ideas and growth. They are willing to take risks to make an impact and make a difference in the lives of others.

A leader in a BRAVE relationship shares their journey of overcoming challenges and pursuing passions during a team meeting. This transparency inspires team members to reflect on their own dreams and motivates them to pursue personal and professional growth, inspiring an environment of inspiration and creativity.

Successes are celebrated together, demonstrating mutual support and reinforcing the team's strength. Celebrations range from big to small, whether it's a team member's child graduating preschool, a gender reveal, a client success story, increased agency revenues, team member recognition, and much more.

Celebrating together builds solid, healthy relationships, creating an environment where life's highs and lows are shared. While we may not traditionally celebrate life's challenges—such as a team member going through a divorce, facing financial hardship, dealing with an ill parent, making a significant mistake in a report, or misspeaking to a colleague—we can still honor the authenticity of our relationships during these times.

Authentic Communication

The key to handling difficult conversations is to be direct and honest while remaining kind and thoughtful. The authors believe in the principle, "I say what I mean, but I don't say it mean." Most people are reluctant to engage in difficult conversations, often experiencing anxiety that can lead to restless sleep, anxiousness, and even panic attacks.

Addressing issues directly allows for quick resolution, minimizing stress, and fostering a healthier work environment.

A manager notices a decline in a team member's performance. Instead of avoiding the issue, the manager schedules a one-on-one meeting. The conversation is approached with empathy, focused on understanding and collaboratively finding solutions, thereby reducing anxiety and promoting a supportive work environment.

When two team members disagree, a BRAVE communication approach lets them openly discuss their perspectives. The facilitator ensures the conversation remains respectful and constructive, guiding them toward a resolution that acknowledges both sides and strengthens their working relationship.

Effective communication is the foundation of any healthy, trusting relationship. When we approach our interactions with transparency, respect, and honesty, it cultivates an environment of mutual understanding and security. No one wants to be left deciphering hidden agendas.

Authenticity offers a refreshing sense of clarity and reassurance. It demonstrates that you value the relationship enough to engage thoughtfully and directly. By intentionally expressing yourself - with gentleness balanced by a genuine commitment to honesty - you send a powerful message: I care about you and our connection enough to have tough conversations, to be vulnerable, and to work through any challenges.

This level of transparency speaks volumes. It translates to the other person as a profound investment in the relationship. This level of directness, born out of mutual respect, lays the groundwork for deeper trust, intimacy, and the ability to navigate differences in a productive, solutions-oriented way. Ultimately, authentic, thoughtful communication is the bedrock upon which the most rewarding interpersonal bonds are built and maintained over time.

As a manager faced with a challenging situation involving one of her team leaders, the organization recognized the need to address the team leader's declining performance in a thoughtful and empathetic manner. Embodying the principles of BRAVE communication - being Brave, Resilient, Authentic, Vulnerable, and Empathetic - the leadership team carefully orchestrated a meeting free from distractions to have the difficult conversation.

They began by acknowledging the team leader's value and

highlighting their past successes, setting a constructive tone, and conveying genuine appreciation for the individual's contributions. This established a foundation of trust and respect, allowing the leaders to directly address recent issues, such as missed deadlines and subpar work quality, while simultaneously expressing their confidence in the team leader's ability to meet the expected standards.

Throughout the discussion, the leadership team demonstrated resilience, remaining calm and focused on finding a collaborative solution rather than placing blame. They also showed vulnerability by being willing to listen attentively and lean into the tension of the conversation, fostering an authentic dialogue.

Importantly, the team leader was given the opportunity to share that they had been feeling overwhelmed by personal matters, which had impacted their work performance. The leaders responded with empathy, reinforcing the importance of maintaining appropriate boundaries between professional and private life. They then empowered the team leader by discussing strategies to manage their workload better and offering additional resources and support.

Following the meeting, a summary email was sent to capture the key points of the discussion and the agreements made, further solidifying the use of BRAVE communication principles. In the following weeks, the team leader's performance improved significantly, and the entire team continued to thrive under their leadership - a testament to the effectiveness of this approach in navigating difficult conversations and building a resilient, connected team.

In an age where superficial interactions have become the norm, the importance of authenticity in communication cannot be overstated. When we engage with others genuinely and transparently, we avoid the pitfalls of gossip and unsubstantiated rumors. True authenticity requires us to speak our minds and share our thoughts and feelings openly, without the need to embellish or spread unverified information about the lives of others.

This approach fosters an environment of mutual trust and respect, where individuals feel empowered to express themselves freely without fearing their words being twisted or taken out of context. Furthermore, an authentic communicative style helps to strengthen the bonds between people, as it demonstrates a willingness to be vulnerable and to see one another as complex, multi-faceted human beings rather than mere caricatures or subjects of salacious speculation.

In contrast, gossip-driven interactions often arise from insecurity or a desire to feel superior, leading to the spread of hurtful misinformation that can damage reputations and undermine relationships. By cultivating authenticity in our daily exchanges, we can rise above the pettiness of gossip and instead focus on building meaningful, substantive connections with those around us.

Our colleagues, neighbors, friends, and family members can take comfort in the knowledge that even in their absence, they are being spoken of with kindness and care. This genuine, thoughtful interaction fosters a sense of security, allowing people to be vulnerable and open with one another. It creates a space where individuals feel safe to share their hopes, fears, and struggles.

In this way, guarding our tongues becomes a powerful force for building strong, resilient relationships - the kind where people know they can rely on one another, no matter what. By aligning our speech with the wisdom of Scripture, we unlock the potential for our communities to thrive, united in a shared understanding that the highest form of love is to build one another up, never to betray. Proverbs 20:19 says, "A gossip betrays a confidence; so avoid anyone who talks too much."

> "A gossip betrays a confidence; so avoid anyone who talks too much."

Authentic Leadership

BRAVE leadership is a powerful and transformative approach that requires a deep level of resiliency, authenticity, vulnerability, and empowerment from those in leadership positions. It's not enough to simply embody these principles oneself - the true mark of a BRAVE leader is their ability to foster an environment where their entire team can thrive by embracing these same core values.

Authenticity involves leading by example, being transparent about your flaws and struggles, and creating a culture of openness where team members feel safe to bring their full, unfiltered selves to the table. By highlighting successes and creating growth opportunities, BRAVE leaders ensure their team is elevated, creating a rising tide that lifts all boats. This approach requires a level of selflessness, humility, and commitment.

When allowed to lead, it is crucial to take the reins humbly yet confidently. True leadership is not contingent upon an official title or position - it begins with the initiative to step up and take charge, even without formal authority. This concept was powerfully illustrated for one of the authors during a conversation with one of their long-standing nonprofit funders. They had consistently supported a key project over the years, as it closely aligned with both their organizational mission and their own. Yet, during their most recent discussion, the funder posed a thought-provoking question: "When are you going to truly own this work?"

At first, the author felt a pang of defensiveness, thinking, "What do they mean? We've been executing this project flawlessly for years!" However, she resisted the urge to be reactive and allowed the words to marinate. Over the following weeks, the author reflected. Once she'd let go of her initial defensiveness and truly listened, it proved to be a transformative experience.

They were not criticizing the author's performance but rather challenging her to make the work her own - to embrace it fully and take complete ownership. The question forced her to confront a crucial reality: if their funding were to disappear tomorrow, how would she ensure the continuation of this vital initiative? Authentic leadership requires a mindset of ownership - of the work, the people, the products, and the results.

Genuine leadership transcends merely managing tasks and projects - it demands a deeper level of investment, creativity, and a steadfast commitment to building and empowering the people around you.

A leader's greatest success lies not in personal accolades but in cultivating a culture of ownership, initiative, and collective achievement. When we embrace that mindset, we unlock the true transformative power of leadership, inspiring others to rise up and own the work alongside us.

Fear-Less BRAVE Reflection

Notes

I experience freedom in Authenticity when I:

_____

_____

_____

_____

_____

_____

_____

_____

_____

_____

BRAVE: *Vulnerable*

There is great strength to be found in vulnerability. While it may seem counterintuitive, allowing ourselves to be open, honest, and emotionally exposed can actually be a profound source of personal power. When we dare to show our authentic selves, we shed the masks and facades that so often keep us isolated and disconnected from others.

Vulnerability requires us to let down our guard and take off the armor. This can feel terrifying. But in that raw state, we become more real, more human. We connect on a deeper level with those around us, building trust, intimacy, and understanding. And this vulnerability, this willingness to be seen taps into an inner resilience.

Being open about our fears, flaws, and struggles demonstrates a profound self-acceptance that inspires and uplifts others. Vulnerability is not a weakness but rather the courage to show up and be fully present, no matter how messy or imperfect. In our most vulnerable moments, we find our greatest capacity for growth, connection, and authentic living.

Vulnerability: Mental Health

Depression and anxiety are two of the most prevalent mental health issues that people face, impacting a significant portion of the population. Researchers estimate that one in five individuals will grapple with depression at some point in their lifetime, a staggering statistic that underscores the widespread nature of this debilitating condition (Wang et al., 2020). When depression takes hold, even the most basic daily tasks can feel insurmountable.

Simple acts like getting out of bed, showering, or focusing at work become Herculean feats. The world can start to feel bleak and joyless, with the constant struggle for survival overshadowing any sense of purpose or meaning. This is the harsh reality for those suffering from depression - a mental health challenge that robs them of their zest for life.

Compounding the issue, anxiety disorders also afflict approximately one in three people over the course of their lifetime (NIMH, Anxiety Disorders). Anxiety can be a truly crippling experience. Relentless worry, fear, and distress take a devastating toll. Those living with an anxiety disorder find their lives severely impacted, as the intense feelings of unease and dread disrupt their abilities to work, socialize, and engage in everyday activities.

> By speaking up and sharing our experiences, we chip away at the isolating silence that often surrounds mental health, letting others know they are not alone.

The constant state of hypervigilance and anticipation can make even the simplest tasks feel insurmountable, further exacerbating the sense of helplessness and loss of control.

Navigating mental health challenges while also fulfilling daily obligations can be an incredibly vulnerable experience in itself, but doing so in the workplace adds an entirely new layer of complexity and exposure. Something so deeply personal, so intrinsically tied to your inner world and emotional well-being, is suddenly thrust into a public sphere where there are often stigmas surrounding mental health.

It takes immense courage to be open about your mental health struggles in a work environment. There may be concerns about how it will impact perceptions, opportunities, and even job security. However, this vulnerability, while daunting, can also be a strength.

By speaking up and sharing our experiences, we chip away at the isolating silence that often surrounds mental health, letting others know they are not alone. You never know who else in your workplace may be privately grappling with similar challenges, yearning for that sense of community and validation.

If we can foster more open, empathetic dialogues about mental health, we may be able to reduce the shame and stigma that so often causes people to suffer in silence. It's a delicate balance, requiring a supportive, trusted circle and an abundance of self-compassion. But by embracing our vulnerability with courage and grace, we not only help ourselves heal but inspire hope in those around us. After all, the world is made infinitely better by the presence of those who have had the bravery to prioritize their mental well-being, even when it feels terrifyingly exposed.

Maintaining mental and physical health is a critical but often overlooked aspect of our overall well-being. It all starts with being honest with ourselves about our needs and challenges, which can be incredibly difficult, especially when facing a mental health crisis. These struggles can be isolating and overwhelming, not just for the individual but for their loved ones as well.

However, building strong, supportive relationships is key to navigating these obstacles. When we create safe, open environments where we can be vulnerable and authentic about our difficulties, it allows our relationships to offer the understanding and assistance we need. This level of honesty and trust is what enables us to work through mental health challenges while maintaining harmony and balance in our lives.

Similarly, in the professional realm, employers who prioritize the physical needs and comfort of their team members often see tremendous benefits (The Americans with Disabilities Act, Research). By going above and beyond standard legal requirements, like ADA compliance, and actively creating environments conducive to relaxation, collaboration, and social interaction, these workplaces demonstrate a genuine commitment to their employees' well-being.

Whether it's adjusting the lighting for someone with a headache or modifying the temperature to ensure everyone's comfort, small acts of consideration can go a long way in fostering a sense of camaraderie and cohesion. After all, we spend a significant portion of our lives in the workplace. Treating each other with respect, empathy, and a willingness to accommodate one another's needs is crucial for building the supportive, harmonious atmosphere that allows us all to thrive.

By recognizing and addressing our mental and physical health needs, we have the power to transform our personal and professional lives, as well as the world around us. This holistic approach enables us to show up as our healthiest, happiest selves. It's a simple yet profound shift in mindset that can lead to lasting change.

Vulnerability: Physical Health

The realization that your health can drastically and unexpectedly decline is a sobering truth. For one of the authors, this dawning understanding came in her thirties when she discovered that the complex migraines she had endured for years were, in fact, symptoms of an underlying autoimmune condition.

This chronic illness now permeates every aspect of her daily existence, casting a shadow over the activities and passions that once brought her such joy. There are periods where her body simply refuses to cooperate, rejecting even the most innocuous pleasures like basking in the warmth of sunlight, invigorating hikes, or reveling in the power of music.

The things she loves most - the outdoors and quality time with their children - can rapidly transform into arduous, insurmountable challenges that her fatigued, aching body is powerless to overcome. This constant, unrelenting battle against your own physiology can foster profound isolation. The inability to partake in previously enjoyed hobbies and social activities leads to disconnection from friends, family, and the world at large.

The ebb and flow of good days and bad days, the ever-present specter of decline, and the overwhelming grief of losing your

> When you find yourself frustrated by your "failures," remember that you are not alone.

former vibrant health can also trigger bouts of depression, further compounding the emotional turmoil. For the author, this is now the new normal - a reality where the things she cherishes can be cruelly snatched away, leaving her to grapple with an illness that refuses to relent.

Navigating life with a chronic illness can be an immensely vulnerable and challenging experience, especially when you have a captive audience of colleagues, neighbors, or family members. They witness the stark contrast between the "good" days, where you can push through and function relatively normally, and the "bad" days, where it's a monumental effort just to get out of bed.

Your colleagues may see you powering through important meetings, masking the pain and fatigue, while your loved ones hear you crying yourself to sleep, overwhelmed. This visibility of your illness and the unpredictability of your condition can feel like you've lost any semblance of control over your own body and life. It's a heavy burden to bear.

And yet, the reality is that true freedom from vulnerability is an impossibility - we are all inherently fragile, our lives subject to the whims of circumstance. The key is learning to navigate this vulnerability with grace and self-compassion. When you find yourself frustrated by your "failures," remember that you are not alone.

Reach out to trusted loved ones, lean on their support, and don't be afraid to share. The chances are high that someone in your circle is also grappling with their own chronic condition, and your willingness to be vulnerable could provide comfort and community. With time and self-acceptance, the vulnerability of living with illness in the public eye can transform into a source of strength, resilience, and profound connection.

Vulnerability: Emotional Health

Grief is a complex and deeply personal experience that defies the linear, step-by-step progression often depicted in popular culture. It is not a neat, orderly process that unfolds according to a timeline. Rather, grief is a lifelong journey. It's a profound shift in your perspective and relationship to the world that can resurface unexpectedly, even years later.

The sorrow, longing, and disorientation accompanying grief are not confined to a specific period; they ebb and flow. Sometimes, they overwhelm the bereaved with their intensity, other times receding to a dull ache. Grief lays bare our vulnerabilities, stripping away the illusion of control and forcing us to confront the fragility of our existence.

> Grief becomes the journey toward healing. Through grief, we gather the pieces and strive to live a life worth living.

Yet, in the act of rising each morning, of moving forward despite the weight of that vulnerability, we find profound courage. To carry on, to engage with life even as it has been irrevocably altered, is an astounding feat of strength. Grief may not adhere to a tidy timeline, but the fortitude required to navigate its labyrinth is nothing short of awe-inspiring.

Grief is something for which no one is ever truly prepared. One of our authors lost her father, describing it as an unexpected and soul-deep hurt that left her questioning how life could ever be the same.

The permanence of losing a loved one is unchangeable. Grief becomes the journey toward healing. Through grief, we gather the pieces and strive to live a life worth living. Skipping the grieving process is not an option.

We often hear that grief comes in stages, and while this is true, no amount of preparation can fully equip someone for the experience. Grief often manifests in small, unexpected moments—a familiar smell, a streetlight, or an item in the grocery store can trigger memories and bring the pain rushing back like a punch to the gut.

Yet, by embracing bravery, we continue to walk through grief with resilience, allowing ourselves time to heal and move forward. Through authenticity, we express our true feelings and share personal stories and memories. This vulnerability empowers us.

Just three days before one author's beloved father passed away, he opened up to her in a vulnerable moment, revealing that he had struggled with crippling anxiety throughout his life - an internal battle that had led to significant losses and missed opportunities.

After serving his country for four years in the Navy, the author's father returned home to a promising job prospect that his father had arranged. All he needed to do was attend an in-person interview for the role. It was a position he believed could have dramatically altered the trajectory of his life. Yet, paralyzed by the debilitating anxiety that had haunted him, the author's father found himself circling the block six times, ultimately missing the critical meeting and losing out.

Years later, the author's own adult son confided in her about his struggles with anxiety and fear regarding a new, exciting job opening. Recalling her father's poignant story, the author encouraged her son to find the inner strength to walk through those doors and seize the chance to change the course of his life.

Through life's biggest challenges and most profound moments of vulnerability, we often uncover our greatest rewards and discover our truest, most authentic selves. The author's deeply moving tale serves as a powerful reminder that even in the depths of grief, we can find the courage to overcome our fears and unlock our fullest potential.

Fear-Less BRAVE Reflection

Notes

I can exercise my Vulnerability by:

BRAVE: Empowered

Experiencing the empowerment that comes from living out BRAVE in daily life is a truly transformative process. It stems from developing a deeper, more profound understanding of oneself - not just on the surface level, but a comprehensive self-awareness that penetrates to the core of your being.

When you achieve this level of self-knowledge, you gain a remarkable sense of control over your thoughts, perceptions, and responses. No longer at the mercy of knee-jerk reactions or unconscious biases, you become the pilot of your mental and emotional faculties. This mastery over your inner workings is the foundation of true empowerment.

By practicing intentionality in cultivating positive thought patterns, adopting healthy perspectives, and embracing the inherent growth opportunities that life continually presents, you harness the full power of your mind and spirit. It's a journey of shedding limiting beliefs, reframing challenges as chances to grow, and aligning your outward actions with your deepest values and aspirations.

The result is a profound sense of resilience and the conviction to shape your life according to your vision. This is the essence of living BRAVE - an empowered existence where you are the architect of your experiences.

Empowered Advocacy

Advocacy has become an essential part of life for many individuals, especially those with special needs children. The need to advocate for basic services and support can be incredibly frustrating, as these should truly be non-partisan, common-sense provisions that everyone has access to.

Why must parents engage in constant battles just to secure something as fundamental as speech therapy for their children? Why do nonprofit organizations have to fight tooth and nail to demonstrate the immense value and importance of their basic human needs services to secure the necessary funding and investment?

At the heart of this advocacy is the core goal of empowerment - empowering children with special needs to become more self-sufficient through specialized education and empowering parents by ensuring they have access to affordable, high-quality childcare. This allows parents to focus on contributing to their families and communities.

Advocacy should not have to be a full-time job but rather a means to an end. It should be a path toward a society that prioritizes the well-being and support of all its members, regardless of their circumstances or abilities. The root of advocacy is empowerment and the hope that one day, such empowerment will no longer require a constant, exhausting fight.

Advocacy is a potent tool for empowerment. It takes courage to step forward as the voice for those who may not have the means or ability to speak up for themselves. Whether advocating for the rights of marginalized groups, fighting against social injustices, or raising awareness about important causes, advocates play a vital role in giving a platform to the vulnerable.

Advocacy work often requires perseverance, a willingness to challenge the status quo, and a deep compassion for those you are fighting for. Advocates must be prepared to tirelessly champion their cause, speaking truth to power and demanding accountability, even when it is difficult or unpopular.

Yet, a profound sense of purpose and fulfillment comes from being a voice for the voiceless and affecting positive change. Through advocacy, people can find the strength to overcome adversity, reclaim their power, and work toward a more equitable, inclusive world. It is a noble and vital calling that requires immense bravery, empathy, and a steadfast commitment to the greater good.

Empowered Moms

Embracing the journey of motherhood with courage and authenticity can be deeply transformative. As BRAVE Moms, we celebrate the resilience that blossoms within us, even in the face of immense challenges. It takes a certain strength to navigate the ever-changing tides of motherhood, weathering the storms of self-doubt, exhaustion, and the pressure to be perfect. Yet, in these moments of vulnerability, we find our greatest power.

By releasing the need for control and allowing ourselves to be truly seen—flaws and all—we unlock a profound sense of freedom. This freedom empowers us to live bravely, to make decisions aligned with our values, and to model for our children what it means to unapologetically be oneself.

Far from weakness, these acts of vulnerability cultivate a profound inner fortitude, allowing us to tackle motherhood's demands with a renewed sense of purpose and self-acceptance. In doing so, we not only uplift ourselves but inspire the next generation of BRAVE Moms to rise up and carry the torch, shedding light on the profound beauty that lies in the messy, the imperfect, and the gloriously human experience of raising children.

Being a working mom is a multi-faceted experience. The authors, both accomplished professionals, face demanding schedules that leave little room for respite, with the majority of their time and energy dedicated to the critical responsibilities of their respective organizations.

Yet, despite the relentless pace and overwhelming obligations, family remains the bedrock of their lives, with one author proudly raising five children and the other doting on six children and five grandchildren. Amid the chaos and competing priorities, these working moms have cultivated a grace-filled mantra that they often share with one another - "You are where you should be."

This understanding, born of their shared experiences, provides a wellspring of comfort and reassurance, allowing them to weather the storms of working motherhood with a steadfast determination and an unwavering commitment to the people and pursuits that matter most.

The role of a supportive, engaged spouse cannot be overstated. These courageous women, who navigate the challenges of parenthood while pursuing their own dreams and passions, are able to do so in large part thanks to the unwavering dedication and involvement of their life partners.

> **The role of a supportive, engaged spouse cannot be overstated.**

Parents and spouses who are patient, responsive, and fully present in the family unit provide an invaluable foundation that empowers these mothers to thrive. Whether it's sharing the load of childcare responsibilities, offering an ear, or providing the practical assistance needed to manage a household, spouses play a vital part.

Their steadfast partnership is an indispensable component of the equation. Without this rock-solid support system, the remarkable feats accomplished by these moms would simply not be possible. The positive impact of their engaged, devoted spouses is a crucial factor in the remarkable success of these inspirational women.

The greatest achievement is the profound and lasting work of building people. This fundamental truth is evident in parenting and strong leadership. As members of the executive team at a large nonprofit organization and devoted mothers, we deeply understand the immense importance of nurturing healthy, thriving individuals. In the workplace, this means steadfastly supporting our team to ensure they are empowered to become the best versions of themselves.

We strive tirelessly to provide a safe, inclusive, and supportive environment, complete with inviting breakout spaces, culturally sensitive representation, and personalized accommodations. This could encompass thoughtful amenities like a private, serene mothers' room for nursing moms or storage spaces to house personal items, as well as offering an abundance of grace, care, and encouragement when team members are struggling.

In our roles as parents, we are wholeheartedly present for our children each and every day, guiding them with wisdom and compassion. We instill in them the principles of resilience, authenticity, vulnerability, and empowerment, encouraging

> **The greatest achievement is the profound and lasting work of building people.**

them from a young age to pick themselves up, acknowledge their pain, and walk bravely toward healing.

We emphasize that it is not only acceptable but essential to express vulnerability and embrace your authentic self. Building people in both the professional and personal realms is the noblest of pursuits. It is about shaping the very future, about raising healthy, thriving children who will grow into exceptional adults.

For one of the authors, the agonizing journey of watching her son succumb to the grips of drug addiction was one she never could have imagined facing. Your child struggling with substance abuse is undoubtedly every parent's worst nightmare.

Yet, this brave woman found herself in the unthinkable position of witnessing her oldest child, during the critical years of his late teens and early adulthood, slowly spiral downward into the devastating throes of drug dependency. Initially unaware of the true depth and severity of his substance abuse issues, she was devastatingly unprepared for the traumatic reality that would soon unfold.

By the time she recognized the true extent of her son's drug problem and the urgent need for intervention, the situation had become nearly dire. She found him one day in the grips of an overdose, clinging precariously to life.

From that point forward, the family embarked on a grueling, seven-year battle, cycling through periods of hope and heartbreak as the young man moved in and out of rehabilitation programs. Each time he seemed to be making progress on the road to recovery, he would ultimately return to the dangerous streets.

Undoubtedly, the most gut-wrenching moment came when she arrived home to find a seemingly homeless man on her porch - only to realize with a sinking heart that the pitiful figure was her beloved son. Recognizing him by his piercing blue eyes, she was overwhelmed with the desire to sweep him up, bring him inside, and nurse him back to health.

However, she recognized that for true, lasting change to occur, he needed to find the strength to overcome his addiction on his own. In the end, the most courageous thing she could do was not let him move back in - a choice that, while excruciating, ultimately gave him the opportunity to take full responsibility for his life and recovery.

The hardest part was calling the authorities, not as a punishment but as a last-ditch effort to intervene and provide her son a chance at sobriety. Thankfully, after years of struggle, he eventually managed to get clean. Now a parent himself, he appreciates the love and immense courage it took for his mother to make such a difficult choice.

Today, he lives a life of purpose, cherishing his family and making the conscious decision each day to remain sober, embodying the healthiest version of himself - a true testament to the power of a parent's unwavering support and the human capacity for resilience in the face of the most unimaginable challenges.

Empowered Opportunities

We define our organizational leadership structure as "chains of opportunity," moving away from conventional terms like organizational hierarchy. Our approach embraces bottom-to-top leadership, fostering dynamic and interconnected relationships. This philosophy centers on linking team members and leaders together.

Chains of opportunity can foster a positive relationship between bottom-to-top and servant leadership. When employees are viewed not just as cogs in the machine but as unique contributors to the environment, it cultivates a culture of mutual respect and shared purpose. Supervisors who adopt a servant leadership approach, prioritizing the growth and development of their team members, empower individuals at all levels to actively participate in the organization's success.

This mentality trickles up as empowered employees feel valued, motivated, and inspired to go above and beyond. In turn, their innovative ideas and passionate commitment have a direct, positive impact on the organization's trajectory. Conversely, rigidly maintaining a top-down hierarchy can stifle creativity, discourage initiative, and leave employees feeling disengaged.

But by recognizing each person's capacity to lead from where they are, companies unlock a wellspring of untapped potential. Providing clear pathways for advancement and actively investing in people's professional development demonstrates that the organization sees them as indispensable assets, not just expendable resources.

This cultivates a reciprocal cycle where team members contribute their unique skills and perspectives, strengthening the company. Embracing chains of opportunity fueled by servant leadership transforms the workplace into a collaborative, dynamic environment where everyone has a stake in collective success.

These chains of opportunity are forged by leaders and team members united by shared visions and goals. This diversity facilitates a rich exchange of insights, enabling individuals to explore various options and identify the best solutions for their needs.

> Embracing chains of opportunity fueled by servant leadership transforms the workplace into a collaborative, dynamic environment where everyone has a stake in collective success.

Whether decisions are made independently or through collaborative input, the process is enriched by the multitude of perspectives within the chain. Ultimately, chains of opportunity empower individuals to learn from one another.

Embracing BRAVE in Daily Life | 67

Fear-Less BRAVE Reflection Notes

I am most Empowered when:

BRAVE: Pursuit

Pursuing a life of BRAVE - being Resilient, Authentic, Vulnerable, and Empowered - is about embracing your true self and courageously living in alignment with your deepest passions and values. Doing the right thing when nobody is looking is truly a testament to your personal integrity and sense of accountability.

It reflects a deep-rooted commitment to the greater good and a profound respect for others, even without external recognition or validation. This intrinsic motivation to act ethically is what ultimately builds trust and encourages a positive, nurturing environment for all.

It's about an unwavering dedication to doing what is morally right, not because you'll be rewarded or praised for it, but because you know it is right. This moral compass, this internal drive to be honest, fair, and considerate of others, lays the foundation for a more ethical culture and community. When we make the right choices, we contribute to a strength-based environment of mutual respect, accountability, and trust.

When nobody is watching, our true character is revealed. This concept is vital, both in our personal and professional lives. This principle manifests itself in a myriad of ways, from the seemingly insignificant to the more consequential. For instance, tidying up a shared workspace after others have left it in disarray or restocking supplies without being asked.

On a larger scale, it could mean mustering the courage to admit a mistake. Resisting the temptation to misuse or even outright steal organizational resources, such as office equipment, company funds, or intellectual property, also falls under this banner of ethical behavior.

Ultimately, this concept speaks to the core of an individual's character - their willingness to do the right thing, even when acting in their self-interest may be easier or more advantageous. It is a testament to our principles, values, and commitment to maintaining the highest standards of integrity, regardless of whether the spotlight is shining.

Character is often considered an innate quality that cannot be easily taught or instilled through training. While skills and organizational procedures can be learned, and a company's culture can influence behavior to some extent, the core values that drive someone to do the right thing come from within.

Even more impactful, however, are the occasions when people demonstrate integrity. Someone who openly shared a mistake they had made, despite the potential for embarrassment or shame. Rather than trying to sweep the issue under the rug or make excuses, this individual took full responsibility, acknowledging the error and its consequences with remarkable honesty.

In doing so, they created an opportunity for the team to collaboratively work through the problem, drawing on our collective wisdom and problem-solving skills to arrive at an ethical solution. By choosing transparency over concealment, this person reinforced the trust the team has in one another.

It was a potent reminder that when we create an environment where people feel safe to admit their mistakes, we empower each other to learn, grow, and perform at a higher level. Integrity is not about perfection but about having the courage to confront our shortcomings head-on. Experiences like this underscore just how vital it is to cultivate a culture where honesty, accountability, and a commitment to doing the right thing are the bedrock upon which all our efforts are built.

This selfless commitment to integrity is a true testament to our values. It is this quiet fortitude, this willingness to do good for goodness' sake, that ultimately inspires others and elevates the collective moral fiber of the organization. The person who does the right thing when nobody is watching stands tall as a beacon of authentic leadership and an exemplar of the principles we aspire to uphold.

These are the types of people who truly make the world better for everyone. While these small gestures may seem insignificant in the grand scheme of things, they add up to create a culture defined by mutual respect, accountability, and pride. It starts with fully accepting and embracing the unique individual you were born to be. By tapping into your innate strengths, talents, and gifts, you can begin to ignite the flames of purpose within.

Lean into the things that set your soul on fire with joy and wonder - the activities, hobbies, or experiences that make you feel alive and fulfilled. Dare to be vulnerable and authentic, shedding the masks and personas you may have adopted to fit in or please others. Vulnerability takes tremendous courage, but it's the pathway to genuine connection and self-actualization.

And as you peel back the layers and show up as your truest self, you'll cultivate personal empowerment. You'll learn to trust your inner wisdom, honor your needs, and take bold action toward your most cherished dreams and aspirations.

Pursuing BRAVE is about reclaiming your birthright to live a life of passion, purpose, and profound self-expression. It's about having the audacity to chase the joys of your world and let your light shine brightly, no matter what. When you embrace the BRAVE way of being, you unlock your greatest potential and begin to truly thrive.

Pursuing your BRAVE unapologetically is a powerful and transformative journey that allows you to fully embrace your authentic self. When you

> Pursuing BRAVE is about reclaiming your birthright to live a life of passion, purpose, and profound self-expression.

courageously step into your bravery, you unlock a wellspring of resilience. It takes great courage to peel back the layers of societal expectations and internal doubts to reveal the true essence of who you are.

But in doing so, you grant yourself the empowerment to live each day with unwavering conviction. You are free to blaze your own trail and live the life you were destined for. This bravery is not a one-time event but an ongoing practice of self-acceptance and self-trust.

Each time you silence your inner critic and choose to live BRAVE, you grow stronger. The path may not always be easy, but the rewards of living an unapologetically BRAVE life are immeasurable. It permeates every aspect of your existence, bolstering your relationships, career, health, and overall sense of fulfillment. So take that first courageous step and watch your authentic, resilient self blossom into the future you've always envisioned.

Be committed to self-improvement, embracing challenges, and maintaining a positive mindset. Set clear goals, seek feedback, and learn from failures while also prioritizing self-care and healthy relationships. Cultivating resilience and adaptability will empower you to navigate obstacles and thrive in various aspects of life.

Resilient living is the ability to adapt, recover, and thrive amid challenges and adversities in life. Practicing resilience involves prioritizing self-care, embracing change, learning from setbacks, and maintaining hope for the future. Resilient living empowers individuals to navigate life's uncertainties more effectively, enhancing overall well-being and personal growth.

Authentic living involves being true to oneself, aligning actions and values, and embracing individuality without succumbing to societal pressures or expectations. It requires self-reflection, honesty, and courage to express thoughts and emotions genuinely. By cultivating authenticity, individuals foster deeper connections, pursue passions, and enhance overall well-being, leading to a more fulfilling and meaningful life.

Vulnerable people exhibit authenticity and openness about their own challenges and emotions, fostering trust and connection with their circle. They create an environment where individuals feel safe to express their ideas and concerns, ultimately promoting collaboration and innovation. This leadership approach can enhance resilience within relationships, as these brave seekers demonstrate that strength lies in acknowledging our limitations and seeking support.

Empowered seekers embrace their true selves while celebrating diversity, fostering community, and prioritizing wellness. They create a harmonious balance that enriches individual and collective experiences.

It's truly awe-inspiring to consider how the divine hand of God carefully and intentionally crafted you, knitting you together with meticulous precision. Before you drew your first breath, He had already envisioned the remarkable qualities defining your unique identity and purpose.

Every intricate detail of your being - from the color of your eyes to the unique fingerprints that distinguish you, from the natural talents and gifts that set you apart to the compassionate spirit that shapes your character - was lovingly designed by the Creator. And it's no coincidence that you, in particular, have been endowed with such an abundance of kindness, empathy, and an overall amazing nature.

These superpowers make you the incredible human being you are, superpowers that were meticulously woven into the fabric of your soul long before you emerged into this world. When you embrace the truth of your divinely crafted identity and walk confidently in the remarkable attributes that define you, you unlock the fullness of your potential and shine as a beacon of light to all those around you.

Being unapologetically you is your greatest superpower.

Message *from the authors*

Michelle- Co-Author of BRAVE Leadership and Pursuit of BRAVE. I am honored to partner with Jacqui Banta, both with our books and in our daily lives. We bring unique perspectives and strengths to our roles as the Executive Leadership Team within our organization.

I have worked with many partners, teams, and peers in my career, but this experience has proven that what Jacqui and I have created is unique and special. We share vision and passion and are intrinsically motivated to be our best and give our all! I am confident that through The Pursuit of BRAVE, others can recreate this.

I am a proud mother of five children. Each of my children has taught me how to love, trust, grow, and nurture. I am a birth mom, having chosen adoption for my daughter when I was sixteen years old. Through life's challenges and celebrations, I have become the mom, woman, leader, friend, wife, and author I am grateful to be today.

I hope by sharing our insights and journeys through The Pursuit of BRAVE, others can be inspired to step up, lean in, escape their comfort zones, embrace difficult circumstances, ignite their passion and fire, and embrace the principles of BRAVE... Be Resilient, Authentic, Vulnerable, and Empowered. Be BRAVE!

Jacquilyn- Co-Author of BRAVE Leadership and Pursuit of BRAVE. Through my transformative years working alongside the ever-inspiring Michelle, I've wholeheartedly embraced the BRAVE leadership qualities in ways I never imagined possible. By staying true to my authentic self and leading with a servant's heart, I've discovered a powerful launchpad to unleash my full potential and harness my most impactful leadership abilities. Empowering other leaders and helping them identify and leverage their unique innate talents has become my driving passion, perfectly aligning with my deep belief in a strengths-based, person-centered approach. While no earthly leader embodies flawless perfection, Jesus stands as the ultimate exemplar of servant leadership, consistently placing the needs of others before His own. His profound example serves as my unwavering guide, informing my decisions, shaping my community engagement, and fueling my steadfast commitment to service. The dynamic, ever-evolving nonprofit sector constantly adapts to meet the changing needs of humanity, and my experiences collaborating with diverse individuals have illuminated the boundless joys of discovery, innovation, curiosity, and lifelong learning. Finding a like-minded partner to share in this exhilarating journey is absolutely essential for both personal fulfillment and collective success. While my childhood self confidently declared aspirations of motherhood when asked about future plans, I never fully grasped how profoundly the journey of motherhood would equip me with the skills to thrive as a leader! My five extraordinary children, ranging in age from 3 to 19, along with my cherished husband, stand as my greatest blessings, and my love for them defies description. I will eternally treasure the sacred honor of being their mother and wife. My mind frequently drifts to thoughts of them, underscoring a love that transcends the natural maternal bond—a love characterized by unfailing devotion, boundless hope, deep admiration, and immense pride. This multifaceted love will endure perpetually, unwavering and unchanging, and I will forever remain grateful for these priceless gifts I vow never to take for granted.

Fear-Less BRAVE Reflection

Notes

BRAVE Next Steps:

Be:

I am commited to Be: _____

_____

_____

_____

Resilent:

I will celebrate my Resiliency in:

_____

_____

_____

_____

_____

BRAVE Next Steps:

Authentic:

I will celebrate to being Authentic when I: _____

_____

_____

_____

Vulnerable:

I will exercise my Vulnerability by:

_____

_____

_____

_____

BRAVE Next Steps:

Empowered:

I will demostrate my Empowerment by: _____

_____

_____

_____

_____

Made in the USA
Columbia, SC
18 May 2025